A
School Administrator's
Guide to
Early Childhood Programs

A
SCHOOL ADMINISTRATOR'S
GUIDE TO
EARLY CHILDHOOD PROGRAMS

Lawrence J. Schweinhart

High/Scope Educational Research Foundation

With a Foreword by

SAMUEL G. SAVA
Executive Director
National Association of Elementary School Principals

THE HIGH/SCOPE PRESS

Ypsilanti, Michigan
A division of the High/Scope Educational Research Foundation

Library of Congress Catalog Card Number: 88-11073

International Standard Book Number: 0-931114-77-2

Printed in the United States of America

High/Scope Educational Research Foundation
600 North River Street
Ypsilanti, Michigan 48198-2898
(313) 485-2000

The High/Scope Educational Research Foundation is an independent, nonprofit center for research, development, and training in education and human development, with primary emphasis on early childhood development programs. Founded by David P. Weikart in 1970, today it maintains a staff of 40 and an annual budget of $2 million from public and private sources.

National Association of Elementary School Principals
1615 Duke Street
Alexandria, VA 22314-3483
(703) 684-3345

Founded in 1921, the National Association of Elementary School Principals has 22,000 members throughout the U.S. and Canada. Its goals are to assure that elementary and middle-school children receive the best possible education and develop a love of learning, to enhance the professional skills and leadership capabilities of all elementary and middle-school principals, and to bring about greater public understanding of the principal's role and responsibilities.

CONTENTS

If you are an elementary school principal or some other kind of school administrator, this guide presents the information you need to develop and maintain good early childhood education programs for four- and five-year-olds in your school. In addition, it presents the curriculum principles that are relevant not only to early childhood programs but also to the elementary grades. It will help you to

- Recognize good early childhood education
- Explain the rationale for early education to parents and others
- Provide appropriate administrative support and evaluation for early childhood programs
- Integrate new ideas about early childhood education into your existing views of education

In this guide, three key questions are considered:

1. **What constitutes a good early childhood program?** A good early childhood program should employ a curriculum based on principles of child development, one that recognizes young children's intellectual, social, and physical needs and encourages children to initiate their own learning activities within a supportive environment. It requires an enthusiastic and knowledgeable administrator together with staff well trained in early childhood development, who receive ongoing inservice training. Each class should have a teacher and an aide, and an enrollment limit of 16 – 20. Teaching staff need to have time set aside for daily

planning and evaluation. Parents should be active partners in the education process, and the noneducational needs of the child and family, such as child care, health, and nutrition, must be considered.

2. What is your role? As an elementary school principal, you should understand the goals of the child development curriculum and help your teaching staff accomplish these goals and explain them to parents. You should provide your teachers and aides with a systematic program of inservice training focused on child development principles and also follow up to see that they apply these principles in the classroom. You should make sure that the evaluations of programs and teaching staff are consistent with the goals of the child development curriculum.

3. What are the critical choices? Every principal who is attempting to implement a good early childhood classroom as well as an effective overall school program grapples with some very important issues. What about postponing kindergarten entry for less-mature children? What about teacher-directed instruction in the basic skills? What about teaching reading to preschoolers? What about standardized achievement tests? What about the dangers of labeling young children by placing them in early childhood special education programs? This guide is designed to help you sort through these and related issues. It is written from a child development perspective but considers other ideas about early childhood education as well.

I have tried to anticipate the most pressing questions and concerns of elementary school principals and other school administrators about early childhood programs. If you have questions about early childhood programs that are not addressed in this booklet, I would like to hear from you. Please write me at the High/Scope Educational Research Foundation, 600 North River Street, Ypsilanti, MI 48198, or call (313) 485-2000.

Many individuals were involved in developing and producing this booklet. I thank Elizabeth Mazur (for helping develop the section on effective schools) and Lynn Spencer (for editing the manuscript). For advice and abiding interest in developing early childhood training for elementary school principals, I thank the members of the National Association of Elementary School Principals — in particular Executive Director Samuel Sava, 1986 – 1987 President Edna May Merson, and the other members of its Early Childhood Advisory Panel: Robert Anastasi, Neil Chance, Carolyn Cummings, Greer Gladstone, Edward Keller, Helen Martin, Neil Shipman, and Romaine Thomas. I also thank High/Scope President David P. Weikart and Executive Vice President Charles Wallgren for teaching me much of what I know about administration.

— Lawrence J. Schweinhart

FOREWORD

The Endangered Promise

SAMUEL G. SAVA
Executive Director
National Association of Elementary School Principals

In the last 25 years, the percentage of three- and four-year-olds attending some form of preschool has quadrupled — from slightly less than 10 percent in 1964 to 40 percent today.

From one standpoint, this burgeoning parental interest in preschooling is the most heartening and promising development in American education since we began the painful, still-unfinished, but essential process of dismantling racial segregation in our schools and society. In my opinion, the extension of high-quality early childhood programs throughout the country offers more potential for educational advancement than do all the recommendations of all the "reform reports" put together.

True, a substantial percentage of the increased preschool enrollment stems as much from the need of working mothers for supervised day care as from any widespread recognition of the developmental value of early childhood education. Also, some youngsters are enrolled in preschool programs because their parents, victims of the "superbaby syndrome," fear that without such a head start, their progeny will fall hopelessly behind in the race for admission to a top-flight college some 14 years hence.

Regardless of the mixed motives behind the upsurge in enrollment, we educators can take advantage of this interest to give more children a better start — not only in learning but in life. Both of these possibilities are within the reach of fine preschool programs operated by well-trained teachers and supervised by knowledgeable principals.

Yet it is the muddled understanding of this "better start" that, paradoxically, endangers the promise of early childhood education. Too many parents and other adults view preschool as a chance to give children a jump on the competition for A's in first grade and beyond; the purpose of early childhood education, in their view, is to offer preschoolers bite-size nibbles of the three R's today, so that when they encounter the "real" curriculum tomorrow, they can digest larger chunks of it more rapidly.

Early childhood education should, indeed, help the graduates of preschool programs do better in school. The evidence is mixed on this: Typically, cognitive gains registered by preschoolers disappear a year or two after they enter first grade — *but they do register those gains.* The problem here is that we have not yet learned to adjust the "fit" between preschool and the primary school curriculum to sustain the initial gains. In comparison with other aspects of schooling, early childhood education — as distinct from purely custodial child care — is still in its infancy, and we have a lot to learn about it.

However, improved student performance in the primary years and beyond will result not from giving preschoolers an early exposure to reading, writing, and arithmetic (matters in which most three- and four-year-olds have little or no interest), but from exploiting the interests preschoolers already have to develop in them two vital characteristics: first, a sense of *pleasure* in learning, and second, a growing *self-confidence* in their ability to master progressively more challenging tasks. These two characteristics, especially if developed early in life, go far toward guaranteeing success in all future learning.

This argument — that early childhood programs should build upon the pre-existing interests of children instead of directly preparing youngsters for the formal scholastic curriculum — is difficult for many adults to accept. Most of us instinctively interpret the word *learning* to signify one of those forms of intellectual activity familiar to us from our own school and college days. "Real" education, we reason, leads ultimately to some skill, body of knowledge, or habit of mind useful or desirable in adult life. Even learning to count from 1 to 10 foreshadows learning to multiply, divide, and — decades up the road — decide whether one's corporation should tuck its spare cash into 90-day Treasury bills or use the money to buy back some of its own stock. Such learning is *serious*.

By contrast, many adults conclude, most of the activities so visible in preschools — the seemingly aimless puttering about with sand, water, paints, and things that go bong — have no payoff in later life; they're pointless, they're trivial, they're time-killers, they're just . . . just *kid stuff*.

Yet kid stuff is precisely what preschoolers *should* be engaged in at their stage of life, for play is the natural way that children learn the lessons most important to their healthy maturation during the preschool years. Far from being pointless, play helps them develop increasing precision and discrimination in the use of tiny muscles, from the fingers to the eyes; it leads naturally into the expanding use of spoken language, the essential base for reading and writing later on; it accustoms the small human — until now the center of most parental attention in the home —

to the socializing experience of dealing with other young humans in a shared, egalitarian environment; it affords youngsters a richer, more varied range of activities and materials to explore than all but the most fortunate homes and most doting parents can provide; and it offers preschoolers the chance to do all these things under the supervision of a teacher trained to interpret the shifting interests of young children — the behavioral cues they manifest from hour to hour and day to day — and to build on those interests instead of trying to shove them in a different, more academic direction.

Thus, the curriculum in a fine preschool program is determined by the children themselves, not by adult savants who prescribe "what's good for them." This does not mean that a good early childhood program is an anything-goes, up-for-grabs anarchy; one of the most important lessons of growing up is that there are limits on acceptable behavior. But it *does* mean that compared to a predetermined curriculum designed to rehearse preschoolers in the three R's, a child's spontaneous interests are a much better guide for sensitive, productive intervention by an adult instructor — and a much more powerful motivation for learning.

These distinctions are admittedly subtle and not easily explained to taxpayers who believe that if preschooling is to justify investment, it must launch youngsters from playpen to honor roll as quickly as possible. But these distinctions are also essential to creating early childhood programs that serve *children's* needs at the preschool stage rather than cater to adults' needs. If parents want early academics for their children — fine, let them go elsewhere. But the school board, superintendent, and principal should stand firm in insisting on a program that helps children do *children* things — instead of pressuring them to do *school* things.

Because making this case to well-meaning but anxious parents can be tough for the beleaguered educator, NAESP considers itself fortunate to have been invited to join the High/Scope Educational Research Foundation in presenting *A School Administrator's Guide to Early Childhood Programs*. Here, in thoughtful detail, is the rationale for a child-initiated preschool program, from an authoritative source. While enthusiasts in this field come and go, some making a sudden splash and substantial buck with this year's book or theory, High/Scope has been quietly and patiently exploring the nature of quality in early childhood education since 1970. Its findings from such projects as the Perry Preschool program in Ypsilanti, Michigan, have commanded the attention and influenced the thinking of all serious researchers and practitioners in this field. I commend this book to every principal and education policymaker who recognizes that a human's earliest years have a lifelong impact — and who wants to help our current crop of preschoolers derive the greatest value, pleasure, and fulfillment from their childhood.

A
School Administrator's
Guide to
Early Childhood Programs

I

THE RATIONALE FOR
GOOD EARLY CHILDHOOD EDUCATION

T oday, numerous carefully designed experimental research studies point out the great potential of high-quality early childhood education, especially for children at risk of school failure. In this chapter, we present these research results in straightforward, nontechnical language, so that you in turn can present them to parents, teachers, and others.

WHAT GOOD EARLY CHILDHOOD PROGRAMS
CAN ACCOMPLISH

In one of our experimental studies of the effects of early childhood education, the Perry Preschool study (Berrueta-Clement, Schweinhart, Barnett, Epstein, & Weikart, 1984), we randomly assigned children at risk of school failure either to a "preschool group" that attended the Perry Preschool Program or to a "no-preschool group" that attended no preschool program; the two groups were almost exactly alike in background characteristics. In assessing effects of the preschool program, we considered subsequent differences favoring the preschool group to be *program benefits* and would have considered differences favoring the no-preschool group to be *program costs*. In fact, from the time study participants were four years old up to the time they were nineteen years old, we consistently found program *benefits*, not costs; we are now collecting data from participants at age twenty-eight to discover if program benefits extend even into adult life.

The study so far has revealed very interesting results. Not only did the program provide an immediate benefit to parents in the form of supplemental child care; it also produced short-term benefits including improvements in children's intellectual and social skills at elementary-school entry, *and* long-term social benefits including reduced risks of educational handicap, of school drop-out, of juvenile delinquency, of unemployment, and of the need for welfare assistance. These long-term social benefits resulted in less need for various costly public services, a significant long-term financial benefit for taxpayers. (Appendix A contains more information on this cost-benefit analysis as well as other details of High/Scope's Perry Preschool study.)

As might be expected, ours are not the only studies reaching these conclusions. Many other studies have verified the short-term effects of good early childhood development programs, and a few others besides ours have examined and found long-term effects. In addition to ours, the long-term studies we consider here are the Early Training study in Murfreesboro, Tennessee; a Head Start study in Rome, Georgia; and three independently conducted studies in New York State — the Harlem study, the Mother-Child Home study, and the New York Prekindergarten study. As shown in Table 1, these studies have discovered short-term, mid-term, and long-term effects of good early childhood programs for poor children. The evidence indicates that such programs

 • **Do** help improve children's intellectual and social performance as they begin school. These short-term effects have been found in many studies of Head Start and other programs (McKey et al., 1985).

Table 1

Significant Effects of Good Preschool Programs
for Poor Children

Finding Study	Preschool Group	No-Preschool Group
IQ at elementary school entry		
Early Training	96	86
Perry Preschool	94	83
Harlem	96	91
Special education placements		
Rome Head Start	11%	25%
Early Training	3%	29%
Perry Preschool[a]	16%	28%
New York Prekindergarten (age nine)	2%	5%
Mother-Child Home (age nine)	14%	39%
Retentions in grade		
Harlem	24%	45%
New York Prekindergarten	16%	21%
High school dropouts		
Rome Head Start	50%	67%
Perry Preschool	33%	51%
Additional Perry Preschool findings:		
Literacy (average or better score)	61%	38%
Postsecondary enrollments	38%	21%
Ever arrested	31%	51%
Nineteen-year-olds employed	50%	32%
Nineteen-year-olds on welfare	18%	32%

NOTE. Adapted from J. R. Berrueta-Clement, L. J. Schweinhart, W. S. Barnett, A. S. Epstein, & D. P. Weikart, *Changed Lives: The Effects of the Perry Preschool Program on Youths Through Age 19*, Monographs of the High/Scope Educational Research Foundation, 8 (Ypsilanti, MI: High/Scope Press, 1984), pp. 2, 26, 36, 49, 96, and 102 and references cited therein. Each finding presented is statistically significant with a probability of less than .05 (1 out of 20) of occurring by chance.

[a]Entries in this row refer to the percents of total school years spent in special education.

• **Probably** help children achieve greater school success. Half a dozen studies found the mid-term effect of fewer poor children being placed in special education programs and having to repeat grade levels (Lazar, Darlington, Murray, Royce, & Snipper, 1982).

• **Can,** over the long-term, help young people achieve greater socioeconomic success and social responsibility (Berrueta-Clement et al., 1984).

As you have probably noted by now, the findings we have been discussing occurred in studies of children who live in poverty and are at risk of school failure. There is less evidence of early childhood program effectiveness for children who are not poor or otherwise at risk of school failure. There is some evidence, however, that a preschool effect found for poor children would also apply to middle-class children, but to a lesser extent. An evaluation of the Brookline Early Education Project (BEEP) in Massachusetts found that after a comprehensive five-year early childhood program, the school problems of participating middle-class children were reduced somewhat. This study of mostly middle-class children had a preschool program group and a comparison group that did not participate in a preschool program. At the end of grade two, inappropriate classroom learning behavior was shown by 14 percent of BEEP's preschool group as compared to 28 percent of its no-preschool group; reading difficulties were identified in 19 percent of the preschool group versus 32 percent of the no-preschool group (Pierson, Walker, & Tivnan, 1984).

Young children don't need highly academic preschool programs; they need developmentally appropriate programs where they can exercise their emerging social, physical, and intellectual skills.

Research reveals that long-term benefits result only from *high-quality* early childhood development programs — ones characterized by a child development curriculum, trained teaching staff, administrative leadership and curriculum support, small classes with a teacher and a teaching assistant, and systematic efforts to involve parents as partners. Such programs may be expensive, but their high return on the initial investment makes them more economical than a program that costs less initially but provides little or no return on the investment. It is probable that poorly funded programs with untrained staff provide nothing more than an immediate benefit of supplemental child care for families.

Also, research suggests that preschool programs that are highly academic are not appropriate for young children. Findings from another of our long-term studies, the Preschool Curriculum Comparison study (Schweinhart, Weikart, & Larner, 1986), suggest that direct instruction in reading and arithmetic — what some call "formal schooling" — does not suit the intellectual and social developmental levels of young children. We found that young children do best when they experience a developmentally appropriate curriculum in which they initiate their own activities with the support and assistance of well-trained and caring adults.

WHY CHILD-INITIATED ACTIVITY IS IMPORTANT IN EARLY CHILDHOOD PROGRAMS

Today, the **early childhood field** recognizes the value of child-initiated, developmentally appropriate activities in helping young children achieve their full potential. The 54,000-member National Association for the Education of Young Children has issued position statements (1986a, 1986b, 1988) on developmentally appropriate practices in early childhood programs from birth through age eight. As exemplary practices, the Association (1986a) lists classroom settings in which

• Adults provide opportunities for children to choose from among a variety of activities, materials, and equipment, and time to explore through active involvement. (p. 10)

• Children select many of their own activities from among a variety of learning areas the teacher prepares. (p. 23)

• Much of young children's learning takes place when they direct their own play activities. (p. 6)

• Learning takes place as children touch, manipulate, and experiment with things and interact with people. (p. 7)

Parents, too, are placing more value on children's independence and initiation of their own activity. Duane Alwin (1984) of the University of Michigan's Institute for Social Research cites surveys finding that parents in the 1950s highly valued obedience and good manners in their children, while today's parents prefer their children to be independent and self-reliant. His analysis attributes the shift to various changes in society: the increase in labor force participation of mothers, in numbers of single-parent families and highly educated parents, in technological complexity, and in urbanization; the decrease in family size; and the change in attitudes towards childrearing, especially among Roman Catholic ethnic groups.

Business and education leaders have also recognized the importance of using educational approaches that prepare young children to become self-directed and goal-oriented adults. Several important proposals for educational reform have placed high priority on fostering individual initiative. In defining employability, the Committee for Economic Development (1985), speaking for the business community, focused on the future worker's sense of responsibility, self-discipline, learning ability, and problem-solving skills. The influential Carnegie Forum on Education and the Economy (1986) echoed this educational vision, saying that tomorrow's adults must be able "to figure out what they need to know, where to get it, and how to make meaning out of it."

Research Gives Us Some Answers

Recent research supporting the importance of child-initiated activity in early childhood programs comes from High/Scope's long-term Preschool Curriculum Comparison study. This study has examined the effects on young people through age fifteen of three well-implemented programs based on different preschool curriculum models — a Direct-Instruction Curriculum, the High/Scope Curriculum, and a typical nursery school curriculum (Schweinhart et al., 1986). The Direct-Instruction Curriculum emphasized teacher-directed activity, while the High/Scope and nursery school curricula both emphasized child-initiated activity. (The High/Scope Curriculum was based in part on joint planning by teachers and children, while the nursery school curriculum was based entirely on teachers striving to respond to the child's needs and interests.)

The mean IQ of the children in the three programs, regardless of the curriculum model used, rose a remarkable 27 points during the first year of the programs, from 78 to 105, and remained in the normal range thereafter, with an average IQ of 94 at age ten. We therefore concluded

It appears that programs providing children with opportunities to initiate their own learning activities have better long-term results than programs that rely mostly on teacher-directed activities.

that *well-implemented* preschool programs had a positive effect regardless of which curriculum was used.

Then, in a later stage of the curriculum study, we were quite surprised to discover that at age fifteen, the High/Scope and nursery school groups each reported engaging in only about half as many delinquent acts as the Direct-Instruction group. Persons reporting over 15 delinquent acts constituted only about 6 percent of the High/Scope and 11 percent of the nursery school group, as compared to 44 percent of the Direct-Instruction group. It is important to note that this study *cannot* tell us whether the Direct-Instruction group reported more delinquency than it would have without the preschool program. It *does* tell us that the Direct-Instruction group reported more delinquency than did the other curriculum groups.

Other studies of preschool curriculum models, although they did not examine program effects on juvenile delinquency, did consider a variety of other short-term and long-term outcomes (Miller & Bizzell, 1984; Karnes, Schwedel, & Williams, 1983). These studies have found that in the short run, Direct-Instruction preschool programs can improve IQs even more than other programs can, but that *this is not the case in the long run.* Karnes et al. (1983, pp. 157 – 160) found that by the end of high school, their Direct-Instruction group did relatively poorly on several measures of school success. For example, high school graduation was achieved by 70 percent of their nursery school group, but only by 48 percent of their Direct-Instruction group. However, by the end of high school none of these group differences were big enough to be statistically significant.

These studies all support the conclusion that direct instruction in the preschool years can lead to large, though probably only short-term, improvements in children's intellectual performance and elementary-school achievement. However, they also present evidence that direct instruction in the preschool years is not as effective as other preschool programs over the long term. In particular, there is clear evidence that the approach has little effect in preventing delinquent behavior and high school drop-out.

The explanation for these negative long-term findings may be that the early childhood years are a developmental stage during which certain experiences help children develop the dispositions and skills by which they later avoid problematic or antisocial behavior. The Direct-Instruction preschool approach may have failed to take full advantage of the opportunities that were available to positively influence the development of young children's social problem-solving skills. After all, its stated objectives were *academic,* while the other curricula in the comparisons included *social* objectives, such as children learning to share, get along with one another, and engage in conversation with one another and with adults. Kamii (1986), applying psychologist Jean Piaget's theory of moral development to these findings, suggests that the Direct-Instruction approach prevents children from developing autonomy, because the teacher is authoritarian and uses rewards and punishments, whereas the other two curricula encourage children's autonomy, because they allow teachers and children to discuss their points of view with one another.

Finding the Balance

In considering how to provide the best possible early childhood education experience for children, we must find the common ground between extremes. Young children will not "just develop by themselves," as some would argue, but also should not be pushed to perform beyond their developing abilities, as others would have it. Young children are ready for appropriate educational experiences but not for early academic

learning. We must consider both the child's emergent abilities and the
child's interests in relation to proposed learning activities (Hunt, 1961).

One example of the current difficulty in grappling with this issue is
the growing trend to require academic performance in U.S. kindergartens. As a result of recent cries for educational reform in the public
schools, students from the early grades through high school must demonstrate higher standards of academic performance. Many states and
school districts have identified various academic skills that students are
to master at each grade level (McNamara, 1987). Establishing expectations for five-year-olds is not inappropriate in itself, but these expectations must take into account the nature of young children's thinking
(Egertson, 1987). Young children's emerging abilities are best nurtured
in programs that allow them to explore their environment freely under
the purposeful guidance of adults who have a good knowledge of early
childhood development. With this basic principle in mind, let's consider
what we know about **high-quality** early childhood education.

II

GOOD EARLY CHILDHOOD EDUCATION — THE HALLMARKS OF QUALITY

P eople who are new to early childhood care and education often assume that its purpose is merely to teach young children letters and numbers — the ABC's of our culture. While young children must learn these symbols at some point in their lives, they will not be using them in reading and arithmetic until their elementary school years. *It is more important for young children to be learning directly through their senses and through physical activities.* Furthermore, since an early childhood program is usually the child's first opportunity to learn from adults outside the family and within groups of children of similar age, it should enable the child to develop a positive attitude towards such learning. In this chapter, we explain how to operate a program of high quality that enables young children to learn as they learn best and to develop a sense of ownership of the learning process.

As an administrator of an early childhood program, you should know the answers to two important questions: What are the crucial differences between high-quality and low-quality early childhood programs? What are the critical components of high-quality early childhood programs? We can look to experimental research on early childhood programs to help answer these questions, but such research does not answer them fully. As explained in Chapter 1, most of this research compares children who attended a program and children who did not. Research of this design can tell us how successful programs are but cannot pinpoint exactly which program elements are responsible for this success. We have considered program quality in light of findings from several of these experimental studies — High/Scope's Preschool Curriculum Comparison study, one by Karnes, and one by Miller — that have analyzed the effectiveness of various curriculum models. And we have examined the findings of the National Day Care Study, conducted by Abt Associates in the 1970s (Ruopp, Travers, Glantz, & Coelen, 1979), which conducted surveys of representative day care centers to assess several basic program features and to make policy recommendations about them. In the final analysis, however, we have relied not only on these and other scientific studies to define high-quality programs but also on the varied program experiences that we and the rest of the early childhood community have accumulated over the years (Epstein et al., 1985).

Our definition, presented in Table 2, agrees with the accreditation criteria of the National Academy of Early Childhood Programs of the National Association for the Education of Young Children (NAEYC, 1984). It also agrees with the definition used by the Public School Early Childhood study conducted by Bank Street College of Education and Wellesley College (Mitchell, 1988).

It is also important to note that a good early childhood program can take place in any setting that has adequate financial and physical resources and an adequate number of qualified staff — in a private nursery school, public school, Head Start program, day care center, or day care home. Minor program modifications may be necessary in some settings, but the basic definition of early childhood program quality applies to *all* programs. Examples of minor modifications are as follows: Home caregivers are more likely to provide supervisory support to each other than to receive it from nonprogram administrators; enrollment limits are lower in infant and toddler programs than in programs for three- to five-year-olds; and developmentally appropriate activities vary with the ages of the youngsters served.

Administrators must keep in mind that it is possible to strive for a high-quality program even when obstacles prohibit the full realization of certain components. For example, a kindergarten classroom with 25 or 30 children can nevertheless maintain a child development curriculum based on child-initiated learning activities. (We are not advocating complacency about large class size, but we do not see this as a legitimate excuse to stop striving for high quality.)

Each of the components is important in the operation of a high-quality early childhood program, but the most important component is the **child development curriculum.** In fact most of the other components directly support the implementation of such a curriculum.

TABLE 2

COMPONENTS OF HIGH-QUALITY
EARLY CHILDHOOD PROGRAMS

A child development curriculum

Low enrollment limits, with teaching/caregiving teams
assigned to each group of children

Staff trained in early childhood development

Supervisory support and inservice training for a child
development curriculum

Involvement of parents as partners with program staff

Sensitivity to the noneducational needs of the child
and family

Developmentally appropriate evaluation procedures

A CHILD DEVELOPMENT CURRICULUM

Imagine that you have a message to deliver to one of the kindergarten teachers in the school where you are principal. You enter the kindergarten classroom and do not see either the teacher or the teaching assistant in the front of the room. Gazing around the classroom, you see children busily at work, barely noticing that you came in. They are in the art area, the block area, the music area — and there's the teacher kneeling on the carpeted floor talking to a boy in the quiet area. There's also a teaching assistant with several children in the house area, trying on "dress-up" clothes. The teacher notices you and beckons. You walk over and join the teacher in a brief conversation. On your way out, you stop to ask a girl in the art area to tell you about the picture that she is painting.

You have just imagined a scene from a good early childhood program. The adults in such a program recognize children's intellectual, social, and physical needs and encourage them to initiate their own learning activities within a supportive environment that is based on a child development curriculum. There are several types of child development curricula — High/Scope's (Hohmann, Banet, & Weikart, 1979), Montessori's (1967), and Bank Street's (Biber, Shapiro, & Wickens, 1971), for example. While each has its own traditions of development and research, they all embrace certain child development principles.

*Increasing Recognition of the Value of
Children's Play*

As U.S. psychologists became involved in early childhood education in the 1960s, they developed early childhood curriculum models based on various psychological theories. Some of these models emphasized child-initiated activity; others emphasized teacher-directed instruction. Some curriculum developers, including High/Scope President David Weikart and his colleagues, began to recognize the validity of theories like those of developmental psychologist Jean Piaget. Piaget's concern was with the cognitive development of preschoolers, which he claimed was centered on their thinking about the physical world of toys and objects rather than about the symbolic world of reading, writing, and arithmetic. Accordingly, many early childhood educators began to emphasize in their programs children's cognitive development as well as their social-emotional and physical development.

A child development curriculum is grounded in Piaget's (1970) persuasive rationale for the learning value of children's play. He held that children learn by actively exploring their environment with all their senses, by thinking about their actions, and by engaging in conversations with each other and with adults. *There's ample opportunity for children's play in a child development curriculum, where children have many opportunities to initiate their own activities and take responsibility for completing them; the adult's role is to help children as they make decisions, not to make all the decisions for them.* The adults do not rely on workbooks or attempt to maintain strict control. They *are* preparing children for academic learning — not by presenting precisely sequenced lessons of reading, writing, and arithmetic, but by emphasizing children's decision making and problem solving. Such an approach prepares children for the work demands of both the academic and the wider world that they will eventually face.

Today's experts concur that the core of the child development curriculum is "children's play," that is, child-initiated activity. In child-initiated activity, *children choose an activity within a supportive learning framework created by the teacher.* Children then carry out the activity as they see fit, unconstrained by the teacher's definition of the "correct" answer or the "correct" use of materials. Child-initiated activity is distinguished from random activity by its purposefulness; it is distinguished from teacher-directed activity by the fact that the child controls what happens. As an example of child-initiated activity, consider children electing to paint pictures of their own design. This is not a random activity, because as a framework within which children's self-directed activity can occur, the teacher has provided the paint, the paper, the space, and the conditions of use. Furthermore, as the teacher and children later discuss the paintings, it is the children who describe and explain their work to the teacher, enabling the teacher to label each painting with the child's words and perhaps ask the child to elaborate his or her response by telling a story about the painting that the teacher writes down.

The primary alternative to child-initiated activity is teacher-directed instruction, which is virtually synonymous with formal schooling in the minds of many people. *It is important for administrators to understand that the elements of teacher-directed instruction — lectures, teacher-centered discussions, and paperwork — all of which are standard practices in the nation's public schools, are largely inappropriate when young children are involved.*

Some Principles of Child-Initiated Activity

Drawing on early childhood development theory, research, and practice, we can state several interrelated principles that distinguish child-initiated activity:

Child-initiated activity acknowledges both the developmental limits of young children and their potential for learning. At one extreme are some educational thinkers who overlook the value of early childhood education, believing that the developmental limits of young children preclude meaningful learning outside their homes. At the other extreme are those who virtually deny any developmental limits of young children, holding that children can learn anything, including reading, writing, and arithmetic, if it is organized in small steps.

The best early childhood learning activities are child-initiated, developmentally appropriate, and open-ended. They are *child-initiated* to take advantage of children's curiosity and motivation to learn from such activities. They are *developmentally appropriate*, meaning they are matched to children's interests and abilities, neither too easy nor too difficult. They are *open-ended* in that they allow for more than one correct response or way of acting, a characteristic found more often than not in real-life situations.

Open communication between teacher and child and among children broadens children's perspectives as they learn to share ideas that are not directly imposed on them by the teacher. A body of research on teaching and childrearing has pointed to the superiority of a "democratic," or "authoritative," style of teaching or childrearing that is an alternative to both "authoritarian" and "permissive" styles (Baumrind, 1971). Piaget explained that as children grow up, they learn to take on the perspectives of other people, particularly their peers, if given the opportunity to do so. If they mainly interact with highly authoritarian adults, they will not learn the balanced give-and-take that is essential in much human interaction (Piaget, 1932).

The way adults and children communicate says a lot about the quality of an early childhood program.

Low Enrollment Limits

It is essential to maintain the favorable staff-child ratio and small group-size that are hallmarks of high-quality early childhood programs. According to the National Day Care study, three- to five-year-olds develop best in classes with enrollment limits of 16 to 20 children with 2 adults present — a teacher/caregiver and an assistant. The study found that children in these groups, as compared to those in larger groups, received more staff attention; engaged more frequently in reflection, in initiation of conversation, and in cooperation; engaged less frequently in aimless wandering; exhibited less noninvolvement during free play; and experienced significantly greater improvement in knowledge and skills (Ruopp et al., 1979, pp. 84–97; Travers & Goodson, 1980, pp. 101–217).

The National Day Care study found that for three- to five-year-olds with 2 adults in the classroom, an enrollment limit of 20 is required for children to merely maintain a normal rate of development of knowledge and skills (Ruopp et al., 1979, pp. 93–95). Such an enrollment limit therefore seems appropriate to programs for children of average or above-average intellectual ability and socioeconomic circumstances. However, the same study found that an enrollment limit of 16 would be best for a Head Start or state prekindergarten program that primarily serves children who live in poverty or are otherwise at special risk of school failure. (Although High/Scope's successful Perry Preschool program had enrollments of up to 25 poor children, it also had 4 teaching staff, which is a staff-child ratio of about 1 to 6.) For children below age three, the National Day Care study recommends the following: a 1 to 1 adult-child ratio for infants; an enrollment limit of 8 children (with 2 adults) for children from infancy to age two; and a limit of 12 children (with 3 adults) for two-year-olds (Ruopp et al., 1979, pp. 158–160).

What does this mean for those of you who have enrollments well above the recommended levels? Elementary school principals often find themselves in a position in which the enrollment limits of their kindergarten programs and even prekindergarten programs substantially exceed the limits recommended here. In a survey of large urban school districts in the 1985–86 school year, for example, the average number of children per adult for public-school-run prekindergarten programs was 10, and about half of the programs had larger numbers than this. The average number of children per adult in regular public-school kindergarten programs was 25 (Schweinhart & Mazur, 1987).

In such circumstances, you should still encourage your teachers to emphasize child-initiated, developmentally appropriate activities, even though it is a more difficult task; your staff will need strong administrative support. You might encourage them to invite parents to assist them in the classroom. There may be older students or elderly persons in the community who could offer classroom support. Such volunteers need considerable supervisory support, but their contributions can be substantial. Ultimately, you must join with the school district administration to decide whether your early childhood programs are operating with adequate funding, and if they are not, you must decide on a course of action to rectify the situation.

TRAINED STAFF

Adults who provide care and education for young children need specialized training and experience in child development and early childhood education. A key set of findings of the National Day Care study established the value of teachers and caregivers having *courses and practica in day care, early childhood education, child development, child psychology, and elementary education.* In a comparison of programs, those programs with a greater percentage of staff with such training produced children who had a better relationship with the lead caregiver, were more likely to finish what they started, and initiated more conversations during free play. The children also were more involved in classroom activities in general and showed significant improvement in knowledge and skills. Similarly, when programs had staff with more years of day care experience, the children exhibited less frequent aimless wandering and, during free-play activities, more frequent task persistence and less frequent noninvolvement; the children also experienced greater improvement in knowledge, skills, and vocabulary (Ruopp et al., 1979, pp. 98–102; Travers & Goodson, 1980, pp. 101–217).

As an administrator, you should recognize that **the care and education of young children is a legitimate teaching specialization.** Familiarity with teaching children in the upper elementary grades does not qualify a teacher to work with four- or five-year-olds; in fact, such experience or training may even be a hindrance if the teacher does not shift to a more nurturant, nondirective teaching style and a set of expectations appropriate to four- and five-year-olds. If you must ask teachers who are untrained in early childhood to teach in prekindergarten or kindergarten classrooms, you should encourage them to obtain early childhood training as soon as possible.

In the long term, however, *it is important that you employ well-trained staff who are certified to teach in programs for young children.* It appears that states are beginning to recognize the need for this type of staff training, and this may help your cause. In 1986, for example, 39 states and the District of Columbia offered early childhood teacher certification, either as an elementary specialty or as a separate certification; 28 states required early childhood certification for prekindergarten teaching; and 31 states required either early childhood or elementary certification for kindergarten teaching (Hitz, 1986). In general, to be certified, a teacher must have a bachelor's degree with a major area of specialization, such as early childhood. Another approach to early childhood teacher certification is the competency-based Child Development Associate credential now administered by the Council for Early Childhood Professional Recognition, a subsidiary of NAEYC.

If and when you encounter persons who argue against requiring such credentials or other evidence of early childhood training, claiming that anybody can take care of young children, explain that such a claim is not consistent with research findings. Nor does it recognize the special teaching/caregiving style required to work successfully with groups of young children — a skill that incorporates and goes beyond parenting skill. True, some people are naturally gifted with this style, but most of us must develop it through training and experience. It is also true that adults without early childhood credentials can contribute constructively to early childhood programs, but they must be well supervised and must receive inservice training.

Another important point related to the professionalism and training of early childhood educators concerns salaries. **Once teachers and caregivers are adequately trained, they have achieved professional status and should receive salaries that reflect this professionalism.** To attract talented young people to the early childhood profession, it seems rea-

Preschool staff must be adequately trained in child development and early childhood education.

sonable that we offer them salaries on a par with those of elementary school teachers. But the average annual salary of *experienced* early childhood teachers today, mostly in Head Start and private child care, is under $10,000 — several thousand dollars less than the average annual *starting* salary of elementary school teachers (Grubb, 1987). Despite these lower salaries, some of the most highly educated and experienced early childhood teachers can be found working in Head Start and private child care. You should not overlook this valuable resource for advice about how to operate your early childhood programs.

SUPERVISORY SUPPORT AND INSERVICE TRAINING

As an administrator, you need to understand and actively support the goals and operation of an early childhood program and its curriculum. You should be prepared to do the following:

• To explain and defend your curriculum to parents, other teachers and staff, other administrators, and community leaders

• To assure that staff, children, and the program itself are evaluated by developmentally appropriate measures and standards

• To provide the program with the equipment and resources necessary for a developmentally appropriate curriculum

• To hire qualified staff, see that they receive adequate compensation, and encourage teamwork among staff in each classroom

• To enable staff to spend at least 30 minutes a day in program planning

• To allocate staff time for monthly inservice training sessions and assure that these sessions lead to systematic application of child development principles in the classroom

• To work with staff and parents to resolve parents' after-school child care needs

Administrators are especially responsible for the **inservice training** of early childhood staff. Such training ought to take place at least monthly to address issues that arise in the program's day-to-day operation. When you provide good inservice training, you give your staff the opportunity to increase their professionalism and to receive emotional support from other teachers as well as from you in their efforts to implement the curriculum. Some building principals and program directors can take advantage of the inservice training opportunities provided by their district's or agency's early childhood specialist. If you do not have such opportunities, you can encourage your early childhood staff to form study groups in which they read and discuss early childhood materials, such as articles in the NAEYC journal, *Young Children.* In addition, you can send your staff to various early childhood conferences and/or education programs at local universities, where they will associate with other early childhood educators and stay current with the most recent developments in the early childhood field. (To help you in such efforts, we have included a list of national information sources on early childhood programs in Appendix B.)

PARENT INVOLVEMENT

You know that parent involvement is essential to good education programs at all age levels, but many of you find it difficult to develop, particularly when so many parents are in the work force. There are no easy solutions to this problem. Nevertheless, we affirm that parent involvement is especially important in high-quality early childhood programs and encourage you to think creatively about how to overcome the obstacles you may encounter in trying to achieve successful parent involvement in your school.

A high-quality early childhood program involves parents and is sensitive to their needs. Recognizing parents' crucial importance in a child's development, you and your staff should form a partnership with them. Being partners means that you and your staff should be able to explain child development principles to parents. Being partners means that if parents want to help their four-year-old learn to read, you can show them how to focus on the emerging language skills that are most appropriate for children at this age.

Being partners means neither being too authoritarian towards parents (for example, claiming to know what's best for the child regardless of parental perceptions) nor being too accommodating to them when they want inappropriate academic demands placed on young children. Being partners means you and your teachers are the recognized experts on principles of child development and should be acknowledged as such by parents — but parents are the long-standing experts on their children's behavior, traits, and family background. When you can help parents see their children's familiar behavior in developmental terms, you and your staff provide a valuable service.

Being partners with parents means you and your early childhood program staff help parents develop appropriate expectations for their young children. Some parents hold unnecessarily low expectations for their children; they do not recognize the potential value of early childhood education in helping their children achieve developmentally appropriate knowledge, skills, and positive attitudes. Other parents have expectations that are too high or inappropriately academic. Inappropriate expectations for children, either too low or too high, may be held by parents of any socioeconomic level. You and your staff have the opportunity to help these parents. For example, if parents drop off and pick up their child at school, your teaching teams can seize this opportunity to talk with them about their child's progress. Ideally, your staff should also meet with parents, individually or as a group, at least monthly to discuss program-related topics. In some cases, staff may have to reach uninvolved parents by scheduled home visits. Because most parents are eager to learn more about child development, you could offer discussions at parent meetings on how to discipline children properly, how to form developmentally appropriate expectations for children, how to provide for child-initiated learning, how to engage in parent-child activities that promote development, and how to assess a child's developmental status and progress. Your active participation in parent-staff meetings can contribute greatly to their success.

Being partners with parents means encouraging parents to come into the classroom. Parents can achieve greater understanding of and sensitivity to child development by joining the teaching/caregiving team in the classroom as well as in daily planning sessions. Parents should always be welcome in the classroom *in a meaningful capacity* — either as informed observers or as volunteer teaching/caregiving assistants.

SENSITIVITY TO THE NONEDUCATIONAL NEEDS OF CHILDREN AND FAMILIES

In addition to wanting to know how to help their young children develop in age-appropriate ways, families are wrestling with many other issues. Consider, for example, that **the mothers of 53 percent of children under age six are in the labor force** (U.S. Bureau of Labor Statistics, 1987). Most of the young children with employed parents need *child care arrangements* for the parents' full work day. If they are in a school-based early childhood program that operates either part-day or for the full school day, they need some kind of child care arrangement for the remainder of the work day. Nearly half of this child care is provided by family members and other relatives, either in the child's home or in their own home. A little over one fourth is provided by nonrelatives in private homes, and nearly one fourth is provided in day care centers and nursery schools (U.S. Bureau of the Census, 1987b).

For these reasons, it would be helpful for you and your staff to get to know the child care providers of the children in your school. These may be providers who operate day care centers or day care homes or who participate in less formal arrangements. A primary point of contact for public school staff and child care providers is in arranging transportation for the children. If school buses are provided, arrangements can be made for transportation between the school and the child care facility. The public school could also serve as a convenient site for meetings of the community's early childhood teachers and caregivers.

When families have both parents employed, parent-staff communication is difficult to schedule and must be pursued vigorously. Encourage your staff to schedule evening conferences, possibly in parents' homes, to accommodate the schedules of working parents. But this problem involves the business community as well as parents and teachers. The Committee for Economic Development recommends that "business develop flexible policies that allow and encourage both parents and interested nonparents, especially those who are hourly employees, to participate actively in the community's schools" (1985, p. 26). Such a recommendation should be applied as well to prekindergarten programs that are not in schools. Try to work out cooperative arrangements with

Administrators play a crucial role in assuring program success. They must understand, accept, and be willing to defend the goals of an early childhood program.

local businesses that would provide release time for parents to attend school functions or to serve as volunteers in classrooms.

Consider also the issue of child and family poverty. The poverty rate among children under age six was 22 percent in 1986. Fortunately, this rate has steadily declined from its high point of 25 percent in 1983, but it is still substantially above its low point of 15 percent in 1969 (U.S. Bureau of the Census, 1987a). Since it began operation in 1965, the national Head Start program has focused primarily on children living in poverty. Today, half of the states have also initiated their own early childhood programs, and most of these programs are aimed at children who are living in poverty or otherwise at risk of school failure (National Governors' Association, 1987).

Experience has shown that if an education program for impoverished children is to make sense, the noneducational needs of the children and their families must be addressed. Children need adequate nutrition, and young children living in poverty may very well need meals to be provided at the early childhood program site. Also, poor families may need assistance in finding agencies and services to help them. Parents who are poor often lack education and may be illiterate. Literacy training for parents can go hand in hand with early childhood programs. A recent evaluation found that Kentucky's Parent and Child Education program (PACE) led 49 percent of participating parents to complete their high school equivalency certification (GED). In a comparable control group in adult basic education, only 15 percent attained the GED (Kim, 1987).

Although you cannot be all things to all people, you and your staff are in a unique position enabling you to offer referral and to serve as counselors and friends to children and families who live in poverty or who experience other social problems.

DEVELOPMENTALLY APPROPRIATE
EVALUATION PROCEDURES

Your early childhood teachers make decisions about children, and as an administrator, you make decisions about both children and teachers, decisions that are based on either formal or informal evaluations of teachers' and children's behavior and activities. Formal evaluation procedures, by making explicit the criteria for decisions, can make decisions more fair (see Spodek, 1982, pp. 523–652; Goodwin & Driscoll, 1980). **The two main objectives of early childhood evaluation are to assess program quality and to assess children's development.**

Assessing Program Quality

Program quality can be assessed by comparing what is observed in an early childhood program to a set of standards for quality. To assist you in assessing the quality of your program, we have constructed an **early childhood program quality questionnaire** (presented in Figure 1).

Other general program-rating instruments are the Early Childhood Environment Rating Scale (Harms & Clifford, 1980) and the NAEYC standards of program quality (1984). The choice of more detailed curriculum assessment depends on the particular curriculum model that is being implemented. For example, trained observers can assess the implementation of the High/Scope Curriculum with High/Scope's Program Implementation Profile. This instrument, available in draft form from the High/Scope Press, looks at room arrangement, materials and equipment, daily routine, content of teacher-child interactions, team evaluation and planning, parent involvement, inservice training, and supervision.

FIGURE 1

EARLY CHILDHOOD PROGRAM
QUALITY QUESTIONNAIRE

A. Enrollment and Staffing

1. How many children are enrolled in each early childhood classroom in your school?

   _____

2. Given the number of teaching staff assigned to these classrooms, what is the adult-child ratio?

   _____ to _____

3. How many early childhood teaching staff members are at each of these levels of child development/early childhood education training?

   _____ master's/doctorate in early childhood development/education

   _____ bachelor's degree in early childhood development/education

   _____ Child Development Associate credential

   _____ some college courses in early childhood development/education

   _____ no training in early childhood development/education

B. Supervisory Support and Inservice Training

4. How much time do you spend discussing the educational curriculum and program operation with your early childhood teaching staff?

   _____ minutes/day _____ minutes/week _____ minutes/month

5. How much time does your early childhood teaching staff have for team planning, when they are on the job but not in contact with children?

   _____ minutes/day _____ minutes/week _____ minutes/month

6. How many hours of inservice training did your early childhood teaching staff have last school year?

_____hours

7. What were the three most recent inservice-training topics?

C. Parent Involvement

8. How much time does your early childhood teaching staff spend with parents in informal discussions about children?

_____ minutes/day _____ minutes/week _____ minutes/month

9. How many meetings with parent groups did your early childhood teaching staff hold during the last school year?

_____ meetings

10. What were the topics of the last three of these meetings?

11. How many meetings with individual parents, at school or in the parents' homes, did your early childhood teaching staff have during the last school year?

_____ meetings per family

D. Noneducational Needs of Children and Families

12. Does your early childhood teaching staff know what other early childhood care and education arrangements their children have?

_____ no _____ yes

13. Did your staff meet during the last school year with these other teachers and day care providers?

_____ no _____ yes

14. Does your early childhood teaching staff know how to make referrals to social agencies for families who live in poverty or face other problems?

_____ no _____ yes

15. Does your early childhood teaching staff recognize children's handicaps and know how to make appropriate referrals?

_____ no _____ yes

E. Child Development Curriculum

16. Are the early childhood classrooms arranged in interest areas?

_____ no _____ yes

17. Do the early childhood classrooms have a balance of materials, commercial and noncommercial, that are accessible to the children and that have a variety of uses?

_____ no _____ somewhat _____ yes

18. Do children in the early childhood classrooms spend a substantial portion of time each day engaged in activities that they initiate themselves with teacher support?

_____ no _____ somewhat _____ yes

19. In group activities, are the children given opportunities to make choices about activities?

_____ no _____ somewhat _____ yes

20. Does your early childhood teaching staff spend substantial time talking to children as individuals and in small groupings?

_____ no _____ somewhat _____ yes

Assessing Children's Development

Children's development may be assessed by tests, systematic in-program observation by trained observers, and ratings by teachers. The various types of tests for young children include tests that screen children for potential educational problems, tests that diagnose the nature of these problems, tests that measure children's school readiness, and tests of curriculum outcomes.

Any test or other assessment method that is used should meet the established criteria for validity and reliability (American Educational Research Association, American Psychological Association, & National Council on Measurement in Education, 1985). In the assessment of young children's performance, two aspects of validity have special importance — **developmental validity** and **predictive validity.** Developmental validity means that the performance items being measured are developmentally appropriate for the children being assessed. At the early childhood level (ages three to seven), performance items should represent what Piaget called preoperational thinking. This includes such intellectual skills as placing things in categories and ranking them by some physical attribute. Predictive validity means that an early childhood measure can predict children's later school success or failure, as defined by achievement test scores or academic placements (that is, on-grade, retained in grade, or placed in special education) during the elementary grades. Over the longer term, predictive validity can even refer to such potential outcomes of the educational process as literacy, employment, or avoiding criminal activity.

Sometimes, assessment measures are used to screen children for program entry. If an early childhood program is not open to all children of a certain age, children must be selected for the program by some criteria. These criteria generally focus in some way on risk of school failure.

Unfortunately, valid and reliable screening tests are virtually non-existent for children under three years of age, and only a handful exist for three- to six-year-olds. A recent review of screening instruments recommends only four of the many that are on the market — the Denver Developmental Screening Test, the Early Screening Inventory, the McCarthy Screening Test, and the Minneapolis Preschool Screening Instrument (Meisels, 1985). Not all options involve tests, however. For example, one option is to select for program entry children living in poverty (regarding school failure, it may be argued that poverty is more predictive than existing screening tests). Another option is to select children on the basis of some screening test that identifies them as being at risk of school failure. A third option is to use some combination of the poverty criterion and the screening-test criterion.

You should be aware that **tests that resemble academic achievement tests, whether they are used for screening or for outcome assessment, are wholly inappropriate for young children in content, format, and the sustained attention that they require of children.** Except for carefully defined intellectual skills, most young children are not ready for many of the skills of reading and arithmetic computation expected in elementary school. **Children's progress in developing academic skills does not need to be assessed before first grade. Early childhood education does not speed up children's academic achievement; rather, it builds a solid foundation for it.**

High/Scope's **Child Observation Record** is an example of a developmentally valid instrument. It relies on systematic in-program observations of young children's performance by trained teachers or observers. It is based on a series of written records of children's performance over the course of several weeks. Child Observation Record items represent High/Scope's **key-experience** categories of language, representation, classification, seriation (placing things in order), number, spatial and temporal relations, movement, and social/emotional development. It has been field-tested successfully. We recommend that it be used only by persons who are well trained in the implementation of the High/Scope Curriculum. (Copies of the Child Observation Record and accompanying manual are available from the High/Scope Press.)

Now that you have reviewed the hallmarks of a high-quality early childhood program, the next step is to see how such a program fits into a public school setting.

III

How Early Childhood Education Fits Into a Public School Setting

Administrators trying to operate early childhood programs in public school settings have many important questions to consider. What about postponing kindergarten entry? Should a prekindergarten program for disadvantaged children emphasize direct instruction in the basic skills? What are the dangers of labeling young children by placing them in early childhood special education programs? Is a Montessori program a good way to go? What is the role of child care, in centers and in private homes? How does good early childhood education compare with Madeline Hunter's educational approach? How does good early childhood education fit into an "effective school"? To answer these questions, you must be aware of the various ideas and theories about the purposes and practices of early childhood programs that we presented in the previous chapters. In this chapter, we describe today's most widely used approaches. Our goal is to help you make decisions about how you will operate your early childhood programs.

Since child-initiated learning is so important in early childhood education and has such widespread appeal in the early childhood field, many formal and informal curricula now embrace it. Child-initiated activity, as we have defined it, is central to the curricula espoused by such early childhood education schools and training facilities as Bank Street College in New York City, the Erikson Institute in Chicago, Pacific Oaks College in the Los Angeles area, and the High/Scope Educational Research Foundation. It has similar status in the curricular approaches advocated by the early childhood departments of the vast majority of U.S. colleges and universities and of the Child Development Associate training being conducted by the National Association for the Education of Young Children.

But some well-known early childhood curriculum approaches do not emphasize all aspects of child-initiated activity. A basic tenet regarding child-initiated activity is that it should include open-ended communication between teacher and child that can broaden the child's perspective as he or she learns to share ideas that are not imposed directly by the teacher. This type of interaction acknowledges both the developmental limits of young children and their vast potential for learning; thus, the resultant learning activities are *developmentally appropriate*. In developmentally appropriate learning programs, young children engage in purposeful learning and make decisions about their activities.

With this focus to guide us, we will first describe the High/Scope Curriculum, one type of developmentally appropriate curriculum. Then we will critique five other leading educational approaches used with young children: the Direct-Instruction approach, the diagnostic-prescriptive special education approach, the Gesell Institute approach, the Montessori approach, and the Madeline Hunter approach. We will conclude by considering how good early childhood education can promote effective schools.

THE HIGH/SCOPE CURRICULUM

The High/Scope Curriculum is a coordinated set of ideas and practices in early childhood education originally formulated in the 1960s and 1970s by the staff of the High/Scope Educational Research Foundation, under the leadership of David P. Weikart (Hohmann, Banet, & Weikart, 1979;

Weikart & Schweinhart, 1987). Today, the High/Scope Curriculum is being systematically employed in thousands of classrooms throughout the U.S. and in many foreign countries.

The fundamental premise of the High/Scope Curriculum, based on the child development ideas of Jean Piaget, is that children are active learners who learn best from activities that they plan and carry out themselves. Teachers and children work together with mutual respect. The teachers arrange interest areas in the classroom and maintain a daily routine that permits children to plan and carry out their own activities. During these activities, the teachers join in and ask children questions that help them think. The teachers keep in mind and encourage various **key experiences** that help children learn to place things in categories, to rank things in order, to predict consequences, and to engage in other actions that promote healthy intellectual development.

Unlike many curriculum models, the High/Scope Curriculum does not require the purchase of special materials; the only cost involved is that of equipping the classroom in a way typical of any good nursery school program. While the initial changeover to High/Scope methodology may be difficult for some adults, once mastered, this methodology frees them for comfortable work with children, other adults, and supervisors. The High/Scope Curriculum has worked well with children in

The High/Scope Curriculum is being implemented in thousands of U.S. classrooms and in many foreign countries.

many countries over the years. It is firmly linked to both developmental theory and historical practice, and it has been validated through longitudinal studies over the past 25 years. Perhaps most important, it lends itself to adult training and supervision, so that parents and administrators can rest assured that high-quality programs are being provided for children.

Active Learning by the Child

The critical principle underlying the High/Scope Curriculum is that teachers must be fully committed to providing settings in which children learn actively and construct their own knowledge. The child's knowledge comes from personal interaction with the world — from direct experience with real objects and the application of logical thinking to this experience. The adult's role is to encourage these experiences through room arrangement and by using a supportive questioning style, thus helping the child to think about the experiences logically. In a sense, children are expected to learn by the scientific method of observation and inference, at a level of sophistication consonant with their development. The essence of the scientific method is learning from experience, and even the youngest child can do that.

Role of the Adult

Children and adults alike are active learners in the High/Scope Curriculum. By daily evaluation and planning, adults analyze their experiences with children and consider classroom activities that occurred that day. In this way, adults strive to achieve new insights into each child's unique skills and interests. Adults strive to challenge themselves by observing one another's performance and interacting with fellow staff in mutually supportive ways.

An important aspect of the curriculum is the guiding role of the adult. While broad developmental milestones are employed to monitor children's progress, the adult does not attempt to teach defined subject matter. Instead, adults listen closely to what children plan and then work with them to extend their activities to challenging levels. The questioning style adults use is one that elicits information from the child — information that can help an adult participate in the activity or that can lead to the child's further activity. For example, "test" questions about color, number, or size are rarely used; instead, adults ask, What has happened? How can this be made? Can you show me? Can you help _____ (another child)? Such a supportive questioning style permits free conversation between adult and child. It also serves as model language for children to use with one another. This approach permits adults and children to interact as cooperative thinkers and doers rather than as active teachers and passive pupils. All are sharing and learning as they work.

The High/Scope Curriculum shares this emphasis on the child as an active learner with historic early childhood approaches, like those of Froebel and Montessori. It differs from these approaches, however, in that it uses cognitive-developmental theory to place primary emphasis on problem solving and independent thinking, while the historic approaches have focused on social development and relationships. In the High/Scope model, teachers continuously gauge the child's developmental status and present intellectual challenges intended to stretch the child's awareness and understanding. In social-development approaches, the child's active learning takes place because the teacher stands out of the way and permits it to take place, not because the teacher encourages it to happen. In some Montessori programs, for example, teachers view themselves almost as guests in the child's classroom environment.

A Daily Routine to Support Active Learning

To create a setting in which children can learn actively, a consistent daily classroom routine is maintained that varies only when the child has fair warning that things will be different the next day. Field trips are not surprises, and special classroom visits or events are not planned on the spur of the moment. This adherence to routine provides a learning environment that enables children to enjoy the opportunity to make independent decisions and to develop a sense of responsibility for their actions.

The daily routine in the High/Scope Curriculum is made up of a **plan-do-review** sequence and several additional elements. The plan-do-review cycle is the central device in the curriculum that gives children opportunities to make choices about their activities and yet keeps the teacher intimately involved in the whole process. The elements in the daily routine are described in the following paragraphs.

Planning time. Children make choices and decisions all the time, but seldom are they encouraged to think about these decisions in a systematic way or to realize the possibilities and consequences related to the choices they have made. During planning time, children have the opportunity to express their ideas to adults and to see themselves as individuals who can act on decisions. They experience the power of independence and the joy of working with an attentive adult as well as with peers.

The adult and child together discuss the child's plans before they are carried out. This helps children form mental pictures of their ideas and obtain notions about how to proceed. For adults, developing a plan with the child provides not only an opportunity to encourage and respond to the child's ideas and to make suggestions to assure the plan's success but also a chance to understand and gauge the child's unique level of development and thinking style. Both children and adults receive benefits: Children feel supported and ready to start their plans, while adults have ideas of what to look for, what difficulties children might have, and where help may be needed. In such a classroom both children and adults assume appropriate roles of equal importance.

Work time. The "do" part of the plan-do-review cycle is work time, the period after children have finished planning. It is generally the longest single time period in the daily routine and is a busy and active period for both the children and adults.

Adults new to the curriculum sometimes find work time confusing because they are not sure of their role. Adults do not lead work-time activities (children execute their own plans of work), but neither do adults just sit back and passively watch. The adult's role during work time is first to *observe* children to see how they gather information, interact with peers, and solve problems — and then to *enter into the children's activities* to encourage, extend, and set up problem-solving situations.

Clean-up time. Clean-up time is wedged into the plan-do-review cycle in the obvious place, after the "doing." During this time, children return materials and equipment to their places and store their incomplete projects. This process not only restores order to the classroom but provides opportunities for children to assume responsibility for doing so as they sort materials and put them away.

The way the classroom is organized is of special importance. All materials in the classroom that are intended for children's use are within their reach and on open shelves. Clear labeling and ordering are essential, usually with pictures or simple drawings and printed labels pinpointing where the objects are to be stored on the shelf. With such an organizational plan, children can realistically return all work materials to their appropriate places and use many basic cognitive skills in doing so.

Recall time. Recall time is the final phase of the plan-do-review sequence. The children represent their work-time experiences in a variety of developmentally appropriate ways. They might recall the names of the children they involved in their plan, draw a picture of the building they made, or recount the problems they encountered. Recall strategies include children drawing pictures of what they did, making models, reviewing their plans, or verbally recalling the past events. Recall time brings closure to children's planning and work time activities. The adult's role is to help children realize the connection between their actual work and their original plans.

Small-group time. The format of small-group time is familiar to all preschool teachers: The teacher presents an activity in which children participate for a set period of time. These activities are drawn from the cultural background of the children, from field trips the group has taken, from the seasons of the year, and from other age-appropriate group activities involving cooking, art, music and movement, and so on. Although teachers structure the activity, children are encouraged to contribute ideas and solve in their own way problems presented by the adult. Activities follow no prescribed sequence but respond to the children's needs, abilities, interests, and cognitive goals. Once children have had the opportunity to make personal choices and solve problems, the adult can further extend the children's ideas and actions by asking them open-ended questions and by setting up additional problem-solving situations.

An active small-group time such as described here gives children valuable learning experiences, including opportunities to explore materials and objects, use their senses, make choices and decisions, solve problems, and work with adults and other children.

Large-group/circle time. At circle time, the whole group meets together with an adult for 10 to 15 minutes to play games, sing songs, do finger plays, do basic movement exercises, play musical instruments, or re-enact a special event. Circle time provides an opportunity for each child to participate in a large group, share and demonstrate ideas, and learn from the ideas of others.

Key Experiences in Child Development

Children's progress in the curriculum is reviewed around a set of **key experiences.** While the plan-do-review sequence conducted within a consistent daily routine is the hallmark of the High/Scope Curriculum for the child, the key experiences are the central feature for the teacher. Key experiences are a way of helping the teacher support and extend the child's self-designed activity so that developmentally appropriate experiences and opportunities for growth are constantly available to the child. They provide a way of thinking about the curriculum that frees the teacher from the activity workbooks that characterize some early childhood programs or the scope and sequence charts that dominate the behavioral approaches.

The key experiences are important to the growth of rational thought in all children, regardless of nation or culture. They are also very simple and pragmatic. The broad areas of key experiences identified thus far are the following:
- active learning
- using language
- representing experiences and ideas
- classification
- seriation
- number concepts
- spatial relations
- time

These areas are further divided into types of experiences. For example, "active learning" is subdivided as follows:

- exploring actively with all the senses
- discovering relations through direct experience
- manipulating, transforming, and combining materials
- choosing materials, activities, purposes
- acquiring skills with tools and equipment
- using the large muscles
- taking care of one's own needs

"Number concepts" has the following subdivisions:

- comparing number and amount: more/less, same amount, more/fewer, same number
- comparing the number of items in two sets by matching them up in one-to-one correspondence (example: Are there as many crackers as there are children?)
- enumerating (counting) objects, as well as counting by rote

The key experiences are not mutually exclusive, and any given learning activity may involve more than one type of experience. Yet this approach gives the adult a clear frame of reference in thinking about the program and the youngsters. In addition, the key-experience approach provides structure to the curriculum while allowing room for new types of experiences. Thus, as High/Scope staff develop the curriculum in the areas of social-emotional development, movement, music, computers, and drama, additional key experiences will be identified. The key experiences assure that the High/Scope Curriculum will continue to evolve and to promote children's healthy growth and development.

Throughout this discussion of the curriculum model, we have indicated its flexibility in various ways. Perhaps, it would be better to call the curriculum a *methodological framework* rather than a *model*. Adults, working within the curriculum framework, establish the context of the program; the children actually provide the content.

Role of Parents and Community

From the outset of development of the High/Scope Curriculum, parent participation has been one of its hallmarks. In the initial period, teachers made home visits each week to each participating family, with the focus usually on the mother and participating child. The key to effective parent involvement is recognition of the interrelatedness of the roles of parents and teachers: While school staff have valuable knowledge to impart to the family, parents have equally important information to impart to the school staff about the child — about the family's culture, language, and goals. The belief that parents and staff are both experts in their own domains is essential to the success of the program.

Training in the High/Scope Curriculum

Effective training in the High/Scope Curriculum has certain key elements. Training has to be **on-site** and **curriculum-focused.** It must be **adapted to the actual work setting of the teacher** (to the equipment, space, and so on) **and adapted to the group of children involved** (for example, handicapped, bilingual). It must also be **related to the culture of the children** if it is to involve parents in some systematic way.

Training sessions are ideally scheduled about once a month, because teachers need a period of time to put training into practice, to share it, to think about it, to see the gaps in their own thinking, to see the gaps in the program being presented, and to make adaptations to their own setting. There is a stress on consistent delivery to the individual teacher, maintained by observations and feedback. Through a national program of endorsed teacher-trainers, High/Scope staff are helping to provide the support necessary to establish and maintain high-quality programs with adequately trained teachers.

DIRECT INSTRUCTION

Direct-Instruction programs seek to make teacher-directed instruction more efficient by scripting the teacher's spoken words and the child's likely responses. As in all teacher-directed instruction, the teacher transmits spoken and written information to children and, through questioning, paperwork, and tests, checks to make sure the information has been received.

In Direct-Instruction programs, teachers initiate all the activities; children initiate none of them. These activities may be developmentally appropriate, but sometimes they are not — as, for example, when flash cards are used to teach reading or arithmetic to very young children. Teacher questioning looks for single, "correct" answers and is not open-ended. The teacher identifies the child's entry-level skills, then presents instruction along predetermined lines, based on these skills. Interaction among children is not a part of the curriculum model.

At its best, the Direct-Instruction approach encourages teachers to believe in children's potential. Direct-Instruction advocates embrace the concept that anyone can learn virtually anything if it is organized into understandable steps. They hold that if something is not learned, it is because such a learning opportunity is not available.

But Direct Instruction tends to undervalue maturation as a major determinant of children's developmental status. As a case in point, Carl Bereiter, a designer of the Direct-Instruction program used in the High/Scope Preschool Curriculum Comparison study, sees his program's objectives for preschool children as *academic*, not *preacademic* (1986). But, others believe that while young children possibly *can* learn academic skills in this way, crucial opportunities for developing their social skills may be sacrificed in the process.

Another advocate of teacher-directed instruction, Marva Collins, the widely known educator who espouses a philosophy of high expectations and "tough-love" in educating ghetto children, touts her success in getting them to read two grades above national norms, seeming to imply that many others can do as well if treated in a similar fashion. The danger of accepting this "anyone can do it" philosophy about academic achievement is that while some children might succeed beyond expectations, others, if pushed beyond their current developmental stage, might experience only failure and frustration.

DIAGNOSTIC-PRESCRIPTIVE
SPECIAL EDUCATION

While diagnostic-prescriptive special education may occasionally include some child-initiated activity, it is essentially teacher-directed instruction wherein the teacher is in control of the prescribed teaching. This is the prevalent approach in early childhood education for handicapped children. Its popularity may be due to the fact that it avoids ambiguities by concentrating on discrete, achievable steps.

In this approach, testing is interwoven with teaching. First, children are tested to determine their eligibility for the program (Meisels, 1985). Next, children screened into the program receive a diagnostic test that identifies skills on which they are deficient. The teacher then directs the child in activities that are intended to improve the deficient skills and that often do, to some extent. After teaching, the child is tested again, and the sequence is repeated. Generally, in this approach, children do not initiate their own activities.

Experience has shown that encouraging handicapped children to initiate their own activities enables them to develop their strengths as well as to strengthen their weaknesses. As children develop their strengths, they learn they can do things that they want to do, so they develop feelings of competence and self-confidence.

Diagnostic tests categorize children, sometimes unfairly, and the resultant teaching seldom completely removes children from their designated categories. Thus, a child can be labeled early in life and find it difficult to escape from this association, even if the label is no longer relevant or was incorrect to begin with. We believe that the use of diagnostic categories in early childhood special education should be minimized, perhaps limited to the single category of "eligibility for service." Michigan, for example, has such a category, called "preprimary impaired."

THE GESELL INSTITUTE APPROACH

The Gesell Institute of Human Development presents, instead of a formal curriculum model, a set of ideas about child development and school readiness. Founded in 1950 by colleagues of Arnold Gesell, the Gesell Institute has been active in training public school personnel throughout the U.S. in child development, child observation, and the screening of young children for school readiness. Gesell Institute training has often focused on the Gesell School Readiness Screening Assessment. For some 25 percent of children, the Gesell Institute expects such screening to result in recommendations that they postpone entry into regular kindergarten or first grade by a year.

While Arnold Gesell's work is considered maturationist, the Gesell

Institute today recognizes that childhood development depends on early childhood experience as well as on maturation. This modern Gesell approach recognizes school failure as resulting either from placement of less-mature children in grades for which they are ready chronologically but not developmentally (Ames, Gillespie, & Streff, 1985) or from a lack of developmentally appropriate learning experiences in the preschool years, particularly among children who live in poverty. A school district using this Gesell Institute approach would offer prekindergarten programs as well as transition programs, either before kindergarten entry or between kindergarten and first grade.

Screening children for kindergarten readiness has become an issue in some school systems because educational "reform" has led to increased pressure from administrators and parents to place academic expectations on kindergartners. Noted child development expert David Elkind (1986, 1987) has argued persuasively that children are harmed by such pressure, both in education and in American society as a whole. While technological advancements have given young children access to more information than ever before, technology has not changed the way young children relate to the world. Froebel's idea of a "child's garden" in

Screening children for kindergarten readiness is a hotly debated topic among today's early childhood educators.

which five-year-olds play is just as valid today as it was in the early 1800s. The Gesell Institute speaks for the early childhood field when it tells public school educators that most five-year-olds are not ready for *academic* kindergartens and that *developmental* kindergartens should serve all children, not just those judged to be ill-prepared for academic kindergartens.

The child's developmental age, not chronological age, should be the basis for his or her grade placement and other decisions affecting the individual educational program. The Gesell Institute has put this principle into practice by using the Gesell School Readiness Screening Assessment to identify the developmental ages of children, although the measure has not yet been psychometrically validated. It is particularly important that the instrument demonstrate *predictive validity* — a high percentage of correct placements and a low percentage of incorrect placements in the populations for which it is used. Until the instrument's validity and reliability are thus documented, the Gesell Institute recommends that it not be used for placement decisions, except on a clinical basis and in combination with information from parents, teachers, and other assessment procedures (see Meisels, 1987).

Postponing school entry a year or spending a year in a transition classroom could help achieve a better match between developmental status and grade placement for some children. Such a match may be especially important in the elementary grades because of the prevalence of teacher-directed instruction. But if child-initiated learning were more prevalent in elementary schools, appropriate grade placement would be less of an issue.

THE MONTESSORI METHOD

The educational method formulated by Maria Montessori in the early 1900s is one of the oldest formal curriculum models in early childhood education. It is a child-centered approach that accepts the special char-acteristics of the developing child and places great faith in children's potential. Particularly during the past three decades, the Montessori approach has appealed to American families who could afford the private schools where it has been provided. More recently, returning to the conditions in which Maria Montessori originally developed the curricu-lum, some Montessori programs have focused on children in less fortunate circumstances.

The learning activities in Montessori programs are child-initiated and developmentally appropriate. The Montessori materials, however, to some extent control the child's learning by being self-teaching and self-correcting. Montessori cylinder blocks, for example, fit together in only one way. After initial presentation, the materials can be used in an open-ended fashion. Thus, teachers encourage discovery and understanding within the limits of the materials. Mutual respect, of teacher for child and of children for one another, is an important part of the Montessori method; implicit in this mutual respect is the development of an under-standing of the perspectives of others. The Montessori method expects the child to become a good worker and encourages independent activity by children. Collaborative activity among children is not introduced until the age of five.

The Montessori curriculum has a solid tradition, an emphasis on child-initiated activity, and a sensitivity to child development. It is a worldwide movement, however, and there is great variation in teacher backgrounds and interpretation of curriculum principles. Another prob-lem is the lack of longitudinal research on the effects of Montessori programs. The Montessori curriculum, ideally implemented, deserves to be subjected to rigorous scientific evaluation and longitudinal research.

THE MADELINE HUNTER APPROACH

Madeline Hunter's effort to translate instructional theory into practice has gained great popularity among educators in recent years (e.g., Hunter, 1967a, 1967b). For the most part, her approach is compatible with high-quality early childhood education, as evidenced by her emphasis on motivation and making learning attractive to children, her emphasis on positive reinforcement, her blending of guided practice and independent practice. However, Hunter's approach ties each learning activity to a specific behavioral objective that is identified beforehand by the teacher, whereas the approach we recommend encourages children to initiate their own learning activities, with teachers identifying the learning patterns to be facilitated within these activities. The early childhood teacher we envision, while having potential objectives in mind, acts on these objectives in the context of child-initiated activities and behaviors. Hunter's approach resembles the Montessori approach in that both emphasize a structured teacher-presentation with a specific learning objective, and both permit this to be followed by a variety of forms of practice, including child-initiated activities, to master the objective.

GOOD EARLY CHILDHOOD EDUCATION AND THE EFFECTIVE-SCHOOLS MOVEMENT

The Effective-Schools movement has been one of the strongest recent efforts to reform elementary schools, particularly those serving children living in poverty. This research-based movement was born of the belief that the school plays a critical role in helping poor children become "at least as well prepared in basic school skills as the children of the middle class" (Edmonds, 1979, p. 28). Yet, as you well know, the search for ways to improve the school achievement of poor children has been frustrating. The family background factors that influence student learning cannot easily be changed, and educational factors that could be changed — raising teacher salaries, buying more library books, or constructing new school buildings (Purkey & Smith, 1983) — have been found to bear little relationship to achievement.

However, by examining the schools where poor children consistently produced high achievement test scores, the Effective-Schools research has identified characteristics that these schools share. Of 13 factors of school effectiveness identified in a comprehensive literature review (Purkey & Smith, 1983), 3 are clearly consistent with our criteria for good early childhood education — instructional leadership, curriculum articulation and organization, and parental involvement and support. Another 3 factors can meet our early childhood program criteria with appropriate interpretation — maximized learning time, clear goals and commonly shared high expectations, and order and discipline. In the following paragraphs, we consider how these 6 Effective-Schools factors relate to the good early childhood practices we have identified in this booklet. More important, however, these factors can serve as guidelines for you in establishing effective programs for *all* the students in your school. (The remaining 7 factors relate to school-wide functioning, in

Effective-Schools research shows that the principal's instructional leadership is of utmost importance.

which an early childhood program might play a part, and are not discussed further here. They are school-site management, staff stability, schoolwide staff development, schoolwide recognition of academic success, district support, collaborative planning and collegial relationships, and sense of community.)

Effective-Schools research shows that the principal's instructional leadership is of utmost importance. This should extend to your unstinting support for adopting the goals and procedures of a child development curriculum in your early childhood program. Just as the effective elementary school needs curriculum articulation and organization, so does good early childhood education. One common element in both programs is respect for children's developmental levels. You should therefore expect young children to master appropriate early childhood thinking skills, just as you expect children in the primary grades to master the basic academic and thinking skills appropriate to children of their age.

Effective-Schools research has identified parental involvement and support as a major factor in student achievement. You should therefore help parents increase their understanding of their child's learning and development in the context of your early childhood program and of your elementary program.

Effective-Schools research focuses on improving academic achievement. You therefore should understand why good early childhood education, although it will contribute to higher academic achievement in the long run, does not have the short-term goal of improving academic achievement in the basic skills of reading, writing, and arithmetic. You should be able to explain to others that the focus of early childhood learning is on physical activities and spoken language rather than on abstract activities and written symbols. If the overall goals of your elementary school are broadened to include this type of early childhood learning, the criteria for an effective school can readily be re-interpreted to include high-quality early childhood education.

Effective-Schools research has found that maximized learning time, with classes free from disruptions and distractions, contributes to improved academic achievement. Some might use this finding to push for more teacher-directed instruction rather than for child-initiated learning activity in an early childhood program. You should therefore be able to explain that child-initiated learning activity is the type of learning time that should be maximized for young children and that it is through such learning that young children develop the knowledge, skills, and dispositions that lead to later academic success. Your goal, then, is to maximize the time devoted to child-initiated learning activities in your early childhood program, just as you maximize learning time in later grades.

Effective-Schools research points to the importance of clear goals and high expectations for work and achievement that are shared by the staff and students. Effective schools have a distinct climate of attitudes, behaviors, and values oriented towards successful teaching and learning. You should therefore be able to explain how such a climate is appropriate to early childhood education as well, if the goals and expectations are developmentally appropriate and center on child-initiated learning activities. You must understand that children who initiate their own learning activities will develop the sense of personal efficacy and ownership of learning that results from such shared goals and expectations. By holding children responsible for their own work, requiring accountability, and giving them the chance to exercise power, your teachers are communicating that children are expected to succeed and that the ability to do so is under their control. You must realize that children who attend good early childhood programs will have many opportunities to initiate their own activities and to take responsibility for completing them; by emphasizing the student's emerging decision-making and problem-solving abilities, a child development curriculum will prepare children not only for the academic demands of elementary and high school but also for the demands of their future careers.

Effective-Schools research has found that order and discipline in effective schools result from clear, reasonable rules, fairly and consistently enforced, and that such orderliness not only can reduce behavior problems that interfere with learning but also can promote feelings of pride and responsibility within the school community. Such disciplinary techniques can work with younger children as well as with older children. This finding may encourage some persons to push for rules that are too restrictive for young children and will lead to unnecessary discipline problems. You therefore should be able to explain that a good early childhood classroom is characterized by the hum of individuals engaged in purposeful activities, much like adults at a party or in an office. Sometimes one person may be talking, but often there may be many conversations around the room. Nevertheless, it is understood that even at the early childhood level, the standard rules of politeness apply and are clearly and, when necessary, assertively communicated to children.

CONCLUSION

Early childhood education — as practiced in the nation's child care centers and homes, and in Head Start, prekindergarten, and kindergarten programs — is not merely the transmission to young minds of the concepts of numbers, letters, shapes, and colors. It is our first public statement of the values we wish to pass on to our children. We say that we value personal initiative, collaborative problem solving, and tolerance and respect for others. These, then, are the values that should be evident in every setting where young children spend their time and have the opportunity to create their own futures.

REFERENCES

Alwin, D. F. (1984). Trends in parental socialization values: Detroit, 1958–1983. *American Journal of Sociology, 90*(2), 359–382.

American Educational Research Association, American Psychological Association, & National Council on Measurement in Education. (1985). *Standards for educational and psychological testing.* Washington, DC: American Psychological Association.

Ames, L. B., Gillespie, C., & Streff, J. W. (1985). *Stop school failure.* Flemington, NJ: Programs for Education.

Baumrind, D. (1971). Current patterns of parental authority. *Developmental Psychology Monograph, 4*(4, Part 2).

Bereiter, C. (1986). Does direct instruction cause delinquency? *Early Childhood Research Quarterly, 1,* 289–292.

Berrueta-Clement, J. R., Schweinhart, L. J., Barnett, W. S., Epstein, A. S., & Weikart, D. P. (1984). *Changed lives: The effects of the Perry Preschool program on youths through age 19* (Monographs of the High/Scope Educational Research Foundation, 8). Ypsilanti, MI: High/Scope Press.

Biber, B., Shapiro, E., & Wickens, D. (1971). *Promoting cognitive growth: A developmental interaction point of view.* Washington, DC: NAEYC.

Carnegie Forum on Education and the Economy, Task Force on Teaching as a Profession. (1986). *A nation prepared: Teachers for the 21st century.* Washington, DC: Author.

Committee for Economic Development, Research and Policy Committee. (1985). *Investing in our children.* Washington, DC: Author.

Edmonds, R. (1979). Some schools work and more can. *Social Policy, 9*(5), 28–32.

Egertson, H. (1987, May 20). Reclaiming kindergarten for 5-year-olds. *Education Week, 6*(34), 28, 19.

Elkind, D. (1986). Formal education and early childhood education: An essential difference. *Phi Delta Kappan, 67*(9), 631–636.

Elkind, D. (1987). *Miseducation: Preschoolers at risk.* New York: Knopf.

Epstein A. S., Morgan, G., Curry, N., Endsley, R., Bradbard, M., & Rashid, H. (1985). *Quality in early childhood programs: Four perspectives* (High/Scope Early Childhood Policy Papers, 3). Ypsilanti, MI: High/Scope Press. (ERIC Document ED 262 903)

Goodwin, W. L., & Driscoll, L. A. (1980). *Handbook for measurement and evaluation in early childhood education.* San Francisco: Jossey-Bass.

Grubb, W. N. (1987). *Young children face the states: Issues and options for early childhood programs.* New Brunswick, NJ: Rutgers University Center for Policy Research in Education.

Harms, T., & Clifford, R. M. (1980). *Early Childhood Environment Rating Scale.* New York: Teachers College Press.

Hitz, R. (1986, June). *Certification of teachers of young children: A survey conducted by the Oregon Department of Education.* Salem, OR: Author.

Hohmann, M., Banet, B., & Weikart, D. P. (1979). *Young children in action: A manual for preschool educators.* Ypsilanti, MI: High/Scope Press.

Hunt, J. McV. (1961). *Intelligence and experience.* New York: Ronald Press.

Hunter, M. (1967a). *Motivation theory for teachers.* El Segundo, CA: TIP Publications.

Hunter, M. (1967b). *Reinforcement theory for teachers.* El Segundo, CA: TIP Publications.

Kamii, C. (1986, September). Autonomy vs. heteronomy. *Principal, 66*(1), 68–70.

Karnes, M. B., Schwedel, A. M., & Williams, M. B. (1983). A comparison of five approaches for educating young children from low-income homes. In Consortium for Longitudinal Studies, *As the twig is bent . . . lasting effects of preschool programs* (pp. 133–170). Hillsdale, NJ: Erlbaum.

Kim, Y. K. (1987, June). *Parent and Child Program evaluation report*. Lexington, KY: University of Kentucky Educational & Counseling Psychology Department and Human Development Institute.

Lazar, I., Darlington, R., Murray, H., Royce, J., & Snipper, A. (1982). Lasting effects of early education. *Monographs of the Society for Research in Child Development, 47*(2–3, Serial No. 195).

McNamara, T. C. (1987, April). *A large school district's perspective on the structure controversy*. Paper presented at the annual meeting of the American Educational Research Association, Washington, DC.

McKey, R. H., Condelli, L., Ganson, H., Barrett, B., McConkey, C., & Plantz, M. (1985, June). *The impact of Head Start on children, families, and communities* (Final report of the Head Start Evaluation, Synthesis, and Utilization Project). Washington, DC: CSR.

Meisels, S. J. (1985). *Developmental screening in early childhood: A guide* (rev. ed.). Washington, DC: NAEYC.

Meisels, S. J. (1987, January). Uses and abuses of developmental screening and school readiness testing. *Young Children, 42*(2), 4–9 & 68–73.

Miller, L. B., & Bizzell, R. P. (1984). Long-term effects of four preschool programs: 9th and 10th grade results. *Child Development, 55*, 1570–1587.

Mitchell, A. (1988). The Public School Early Childhood study. In L. de Pietro & L. J. Schweinhart (Eds.), *Shaping the future for early childhood programs* (High/Scope Early Childhood Policy Papers, 7). Ypsilanti, MI: High/Scope Press.

Montessori, M. (1967). *The absorbent mind*. New York: Holt, Rinehart, and Winston.

National Association for the Education of Young Children. (1984). *Accreditation criteria & procedures of the National Academy of Early Childhood Programs*. Washington, DC: Author.

National Association for the Education of Young Children. (1986a, September). NAEYC position statement on developmentally appropriate practice in early childhood programs serving children from birth to age 8. *Young Children, 41*(6), 4–19.

National Association for the Education of Young Children. (1986b, September). NAEYC position statement on developmentally appropriate practice in programs for 4- and 5-year-olds. *Young Children, 41*(6), 20–29.

National Association for the Education of Young Children. (1988, January). NAEYC position statement on developmentally appropriate practice in the primary grades, serving 5- through 8-year-olds. *Young Children, 43*(2), 64–84.

National Governors Association. (1987). *Results in education: 1987.* Washington, DC: Author.

Piaget, J. (1932). *The moral judgment of the child.* London: Routledge and Kegan Paul.

Piaget, J. (1970). *Science of education and the psychology of the child.* New York: Orion Press.

Pierson, D. E., Walker, D. K., & Tivnan, T. (1984). A school-based program from infancy to kindergarten for children and their parents. *The Personnel and Guidance Journal, 62,* 448–455.

Purkey, S. C., & Smith, M. S. (1983). Effective schools: A review. *Elementary School Journal, 83*(4), 427–452.

Ruopp, R., Travers, J., Glantz, F., & Coelen, C. (1979). *Children at the center: Summary findings and policy implications of the National Day Care study, Vol. 1.* Cambridge, MA: Abt Associates.

Schweinhart, L. J., & Mazur, E. (1987). *Prekindergarten programs in urban schools* (High/Scope Early Childhood Policy Papers, 6.) Ypsilanti, MI: High/Scope Press.

Schweinhart, L. J., & Weikart, D. P. (1980). *Young children grow up: The effects of the Perry Preschool program on youths through age 15* (Monographs of the High/Scope Educational Research Foundation, 6.) Ypsilanti, MI: High/Scope Press.

Schweinhart, L. J., Weikart, D. P., & Larner, M. B. (1986). Consequences of three preschool curriculum models through age 15. *Early Childhood Research Quarterly, 1*(1), 15–35.

Spodek, B. (Ed.). (1982). *Handbook of research in early childhood education: Part V, Research methods in early childhood education* (pp. 523–652). New York: The Free Press.

Travers, J., & Goodson, B. D. (1980). *Research results of the National Day Care study* (Final report of the National Day Care study, Vol. 2). Cambridge, MA: Abt Associates.

U.S. Bureau of the Census. (1987a). *Current Population Reports: Money income and poverty status of families and persons in the United States: 1986* (Advance data from the March 1987 Current Population Survey, Series P-60, No. 157). Washington, DC: U.S. Government Printing Office.

U.S. Bureau of the Census. (1987b). *Who's minding the kids? Child care arrangements: Winter 1984–85* (Series P-70, No. 9). Washington, DC: U.S. Government Printing Office.

U.S. Bureau of Labor Statistics. (1987, August 12). News release.

Weikart, D. P., & Schweinhart, L. J. (1987). The High/Scope Cognitively Oriented Curriculum in early education. In J. L. Roopnarine & J. E. Johnson (Eds.), *Approaches to early childhood education*. Columbus, OH: Merrill.

THE HIGH/SCOPE PERRY
PRESCHOOL STUDY

The High/Scope Foundation's Perry Preschool study has investigated program effects beyond schooling and found them to occur in diverse areas of early adult life (Berrueta-Clement et al., 1984). During their school years, children who had attended the Perry Preschool program experienced greater success in school than did the control group — better intellectual performance at school entry, fewer years spent in special education classes, and better attitudes towards school (Schweinhart & Weikart, 1980). At age nineteen, program participants were better off than the control group in a variety of ways. As shown in the comparisons of the preschool and no-preschool groups in Figure 2, the program apparently *increased* the percentage of participants who were

- Literate (61 percent versus 38 percent)
- Enrolled in postsecondary education (38 percent versus 21 percent)
- Employed (50 percent versus 32 percent)

The program apparently *reduced* the percentage of participants who were

- Classified as mentally retarded (15 percent versus 35 percent)
- School dropouts (33 percent versus 51 percent)
- On welfare (18 percent versus 32 percent)
- Arrested (31 percent versus 51 percent)

FIGURE 2

HIGH/SCOPE PERRY PRESCHOOL STUDY AGE-19 FINDINGS

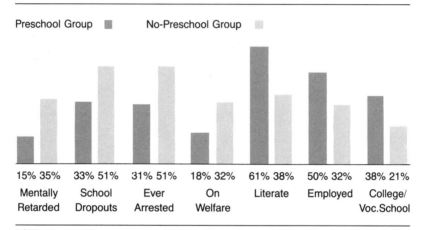

Preschool Group ■   No-Preschool Group

15% 35%	33% 51%	31% 51%	18% 32%	61% 38%	50% 32%	38% 21%
Mentally Retarded	School Dropouts	Ever Arrested	On Welfare	Literate	Employed	College/ Voc.School

NOTE. All group differences are statistically significant with a probability of less than .05 (1 out of 20) of occurring by chance.

The Perry study had an experimental group of 58 children who participated in the early childhood development program and a control group of 65 children who had no early childhood program. These children were selected for the study at age three or four on the basis of their parents' low educational and occupational status, their family size, and their low scores on the Stanford-Binet Intelligence Test. Pairs of children matched on IQ, family socioeconomic status, and gender were split between the two groups, so that the groups were virtually identical on a host of demographic characteristics.

The Perry Preschool program used the High/Scope Curriculum (Hohmann et al., 1979), an educational approach based on Piaget's interactional theory of child development. Most children attended the program for two years at ages three and four. The classroom program was in session five mornings a week for seven months of the year, with home visits by a teacher once a week. Because it was a new, experimental program, classroom groups had about 25 children and 4 teachers, for a teacher-child ratio of about 1 to 6.

Good early childhood development programs for poor children can be an excellent investment for taxpayers, according to the cost-benefit analysis of the Perry Preschool program and its long-term effects. In a book titled *Investing in Our Children*, the Committee for Economic Development, an organization of leading business executives and educators, summarized the analysis in this way:

> If we examine the Perry Preschool program for its investment return and convert all costs and benefits into current values based on a 3 percent real rate of interest, one year of the program is an extraordinary economic buy. It would be hard to imagine that society could find a higher yield for a dollar of investment than that found in preschool programs for its at-risk children (Committee for Economic Development, 1985, p. 44).

The total financial benefits to taxpayers of the preschool program effects (in constant 1981 dollars discounted at 3 percent annually) were about $28,000 per participant, about six times the size of the annual program operation cost of $5,000 per participant. For each program participant, taxpayers saved about $5,000 that would have been spent for special education programs; $3,000, for crime; and $16,000, for welfare assistance. Additional postsecondary education added costs of about $1,000 per participant. But because of increased lifetime earnings (based on more years of school completed), the average participant was expected to pay $5,000 more in taxes.

One year of the Perry Preschool program, at about $5,000 per child, cost about the same as one year in a special education classroom. It cost considerably less than one year of a college education. It cost only a fraction of the cost of imprisoning a criminal for a year. During its operation, the Perry program was a novel program under development without extraordinary concern for cost-efficiency. It was actually relatively expensive for a preschool program, because it maintained a teacher-child ratio of 1 to 6. The same kind of program has demonstrated equally good results with a teacher-child ratio of 1 to 8 (Schweinhart et al., 1986) and has appeared to be as well-run with a ratio of 1 to 10. With such ratios, one year of the program would cost only $3,000 to $4,000 per child.

APPENDIX B

NATIONAL INFORMATION SOURCES ON EARLY CHILDHOOD PROGRAMS

Bank Street College of Education
Public School Early Childhood Study
Anne Mitchell, Project Director
610 West 112th Street
New York, NY 10025
(212) 663-7200

Children's Defense Fund
Helen Blank, Child Care Director
122 C Street, NW
Washington, DC 20001
(202) 628-8787

ERIC Clearinghouse on Elementary & Early Childhood Education
Lillian Katz, Executive Director
University of Illinois at Urbana-Champaign
805 W. Pennsylvania Avenue
Urbana, IL 61801
(217) 333-1386

High/Scope Educational Research Foundation
David P. Weikart, President
600 North River Street
Ypsilanti, MI 48198
(313) 485-2000

National Association for the Education of Young Children
Barbara Willer, Director of Information Service
1834 Connecticut Avenue, NW
Washington, DC 20009
(800) 424-2460 or (202) 232-8777

National Association of State Boards of Education
Early Childhood Project
Tom Schultz, Project Director
701 N. Fairfax Street, Suite 340
Alexandria, VA 22314
(703) 684-4000

National Black Child Development Institute
Evelyn Moore, Executive Director
1463 Rhode Island Avenue, NW
Washington, DC 20005
(202) 387-1281

National Conference of State Legislatures
Child Care/Early Education Project
Cate Sonnier, Staff Associate
1050 17th Street, Suite 2100
Denver, CO 80265
(303) 623-7800

APPENDIX C

RELATED HIGH/SCOPE PUBLICATIONS AND SERVICES

High/Scope Press
High/Scope Educational Research Foundation
600 North River Street
Ypsilanti, MI 48198
(313) 485-2000

NEWSLETTERS

High/Scope ReSource, published three times/year, no charge

Extensions, newsletter of the High/Scope Curriculum, 6 issues/year, $30

POLICY PAPERS

No. 7. *Shaping the Future for Early Childhood Programs,* $10

No. 6. *Prekindergarten Programs in Urban Schools,* $5

No. 5. *Policy Options for Preschool Programs,* $5

No. 4. *The Preschool Challenge,* $5

No. 3. *Quality in Early Childhood Programs: Four Perspectives,* $10

No. 2. *The Perry Preschool Program and Its Long-Term Benefits: A Benefit-Cost Analysis,* $15

No. 1. *Early Childhood Development Programs in the Eighties: The National Picture,* $5

RESEARCH

Changed Lives: The Effects of the Perry Preschool Program on Youths Through Age 19, $15

Child Observation Record and Child Assessment Record Manual, $8

Consequences of Three Preschool Curriculum Models Through Age 15, $5

Follow Through: Forces for Change in the Primary Schools, $5

CURRICULUM

Young Children in Action, $25

Study Guide to Young Children in Action, $10

ELEMENTARY SERIES, $42 for set

The Daily Routine, $8

Room Arrangement and Materials, $8

Planning by Teachers, $8

Writing and Reading, $8

The Daily Routine: Small-Group Times, $8

Learning Through Construction, $8

Learning Through Sewing and Pattern Design, $8

Children as Music Makers, $8

AUDIOVISUAL MEDIA

Lessons That Last: What Makes a Good Early Childhood Program,
   12-minute videotape, $35

Preschool: A Program That Works, 15-minute filmstrip, $35

TRAINING

High/Scope workshops and programs are now being offered for administrators, teachers, and teacher-trainers in cities throughout the United States. Contact the High/Scope Foundation's Office of Development & Services today at 313/485-2000 for information on training in your area. **Ask about cosponsorship opportunities.**